My Storytime BIBLE

Renita Boyle and Melanie Florian

Pauline
BOOKS & MEDIA

Boston

Contents

God Made Our World

Genesis 1:1–25

Do you feel good about the things you make? God felt good when he made our world.

Before the beginning, God was there. God made everything. God spoke into the deep, dark nothing.

"Light!" he said.

There was day and night. God wrapped the world in sky and gathered the seas. There were mountains and valleys, soil and sand. Everything grew at God's command: seedlings

and trees, flowers and fruit, veggies and vines. The sun began to shine. The moon and stars shimmered. Fish swam in the sea and birds sang in the air. God made every kind of animal everywhere. God was glad. It was good.

The Good Life

Genesis 1:26–31; 2:8–25

Do you like being with people you love? Adam and Eve loved being together and spending time with God.

There were no weeds in Eden. It was a perfect garden paradise. A river flowed, fruit trees were full, and the animals and birds were friendly.

8

Then God created the first man. His name was Adam. Adam gave the animals names and enjoyed their company, but he was lonely for someone like himself.

"It isn't good to be alone," God said.

So, while Adam was asleep, God made a woman. Adam was amazed by Eve!

"She's part of me!" Adam said. God smiled because they were also a lot like him. God blessed them and told them to have children, enjoy the world, and take care of it.

It was a good life tending the garden, walking and talking with God. It is good to be together with the people we love.

The First Wrong Choice

Genesis 3:1–7

Have you ever wanted to do the right thing but done the wrong thing instead? Then you know how Adam and Eve felt when they made the first wrong choice.

Everything was as it should be. The fruit from the Tree of Life tasted lovely and lush. They never ate from the Tree of Knowing Good and Bad.

"Don't even touch it," God warned, "or everything will be spoiled."

One day the sneaky serpent slipped up to Eve. "Did God really say not to eat the fruits in the garden?"

"No," said Eve, "just this fruit — or we will die!"

"Nonsense," said the serpent. "God knows that you'll know what he knows."

"I wonder," thought Eve. The wondering was delightful. The fruit looked delicious. She ate some and gave some to Adam. Adam ate some too.

They'd done the first bad thing and they felt sorry. They made a wrong choice. We all do.

The Problem and the Promise

Genesis 3:8–24

If you have ever wanted to put something right but couldn't, then you know how Adam and Eve felt when they left the garden.

Suddenly, nothing was as it should be.

Adam and Eve felt ashamed for the first time and hid their bodies. They felt afraid for the first time and hid from God.

God came to visit them.

"Why are you hiding?" God asked. "Did you do what I told you not to?"

"Don't blame me, blame Eve," said Adam.

"Don't blame me, blame the serpent," said Eve.

"Don't blame anyone but yourselves," said God. "You didn't believe what I said."

And God knew it wouldn't be the last time.

God loved Adam and Eve, but it would be hard to stay friends. Everything would be hard. There would be thistles and thorns, pain and death.

"You must leave my garden," God said sadly.

God promised that he would put it right one day. A Savior would come: God's enemy wouldn't be able to spoil things forever. Everything would once again be as it should be.

13

The Big Boat

Genesis 6:14–16, 21–22, 7:1–5

Have you ever done what God says even when other people think it's silly? Then you know how Noah felt when he made his big, big boat.

Noah lived nowhere near the sea. So everyone said it was silly to build a big boat. Everyone also said that it was okay to forget about God and do whatever they wanted: to lie, murder, cheat, and steal.

Noah believed what God said instead.

"I'm going to start again." God said sadly. "There's going to be a big flood. Build a boat — a big, big boat. I'll tell you how."

So Noah built a boat. Bang, bang, hammer and nail. It was big enough for himself. It was big enough for his family. It was big enough for two of every kind of animal and bird and just

enough food. It was big enough to keep them safe inside. This is just where they were when the door banged shut.

When the rain began, Noah was ready.

We can be ready for anything when we believe what God says.

The Big Flood

Genesis 7:11–24, 8:1–11

Have you ever been fed up waiting? Then you know how Noah felt when the flood was over.

It rained for a long time. Pit pat. It rained for a long, long time. Pit pat, pitter patter. It rained for so long that even the tippity tips of the mountain tops disappeared. Pit pat, pitter patter, swish, swash, swoosh. Noah's boat bobbed up and down, this way and that.

Then the rain stopped. Pit pat.

Noah waited and waited for the land to dry. Ho, hum, sigh. Then the boat bumpity bumped on the tippity top of a mountain.

Noah opened the window. It wasn't time to open the door. He watched and waited and waited some more. He sent a bird to find land. It found a place to nest.

There is a time for waiting and a time for waiting to be over.

The Big Rainbow

Genesis 8:15–22

Have you ever been thankful for a chance to start again? Noah felt thankful when he saw the first rainbow.

Everyone was happy to get out of the boat! Birds flew free. Animals hurried and scurried. Noah's family said, "Phew."

Everything smelled new. A beautiful rainbow arched across the sky.

Noah thanked God for keeping them safe. "The whole earth will never be flooded again," God promised. "Every rainbow will be a reminder. There will always be winter, summer,

spring, and harvest. Your family will grow
and go everywhere on earth."

It was a new start. We can all be
thankful for a chance to start again.

Hope and Laughter

Genesis 12:1-2, 13:14, 15:2-6, 18:10-15, 21:1-7

Have you ever been so happy that you couldn't stop laughing?
Abraham and Sarah laughed with joy when Isaac was born.

20

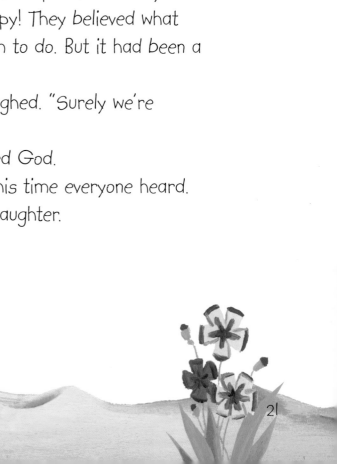

Sometimes you just want to laugh. Sarah laughed when God said, "Get ready. The baby's coming next year."

She laughed to herself, but she laughed all the same.

It had been a long time since God promised them a baby son and more family than stars in the sky!

It had been even longer since God told them to leave home and head for a new land.

"Your family will be my special people," God had promised. "Someone from your family is going to bless the whole world."

It had been longer still since they first hoped for a baby.

God's promise had made them happy! They believed what God said. They did what God told them to do. But it had been a long time.

"How can we have a baby?" they laughed. "Surely we're too old!"

"Is anything too hard for me?" asked God.

They laughed again the next year. This time everyone heard. They named their son Isaac. It means laughter.

A Happy Marriage

Genesis 24

If you have ever been excited about meeting someone special, then you know how Isaac felt when he was waiting to meet Rebekah!

"Isaac needs a wife," said old Abraham to his servant. "She must love God and come from my people. God will help you choose."

So Abraham's servant traveled far from home on a lumpy, bumpy camel. There were ten camels in all, each with many gifts. Each was now thirsty from the long, long trip.

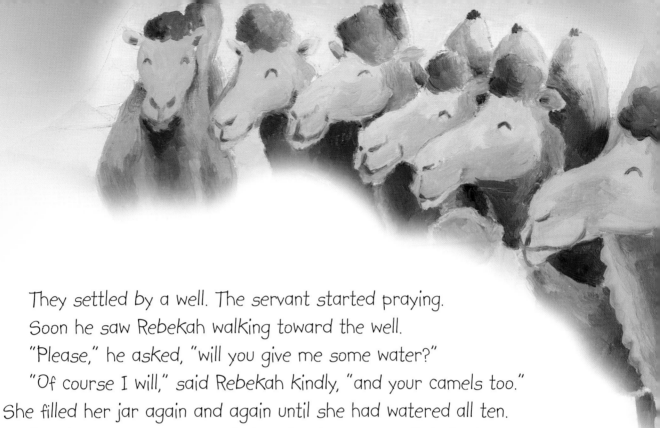

They settled by a well. The servant started praying.
Soon he saw Rebekah walking toward the well.

"Please," he asked, "will you give me some water?"

"Of course I will," said Rebekah kindly, "and your camels too."
She filled her jar again and again until she had watered all ten.

"She's perfect for Isaac," thought the servant. "She's the one
I prayed for!"

Everyone was happy. The servant thanked God. Rebekah said
she would marry Isaac. Rebekah's family waved goodbye.

Rebekah traveled far from home on a lumpy, bumpy camel.
Isaac was waiting for her. When Isaac met her, he was happiest
of all. God's choice is the best choice.

A Silly Swap

Genesis 25:19–34

Have you ever swapped something that you wanted back? Then you know how Esau felt after eating Jacob's stew.

All brothers argue, but Jacob and Esau fought even before they were born. They were twins, but they were not at all alike.

Esau was born first. He was strong and hairy and liked to go hunting.

Jacob was born holding on to Esau's heel. He was quiet and liked being at home with his mother, Rebekah.

One day, Esau came back from hunting with a rumbling tummy. Something yummy was simmering in Jacob's pot.

"I'm starving," Esau grumbled. "Give me some stew!"

Esau had no manners, but he did have something that Jacob wanted. Esau would one day be head of the family and be given God's special blessing.

"Let's swap," said Jacob. "You can have some stew now, if you give me your inheritance later."

So Esau swapped his birthright for some stew and some bread.

Esau knew the stew was good. Jacob knew God's blessing is better.

25

A Slick Trick

Genesis 27:1–42

If you think tricks are sometimes cruel, then you know how Esau felt when Jacob stole his blessing.

"I'm getting old and blind," Isaac said to Esau. "Make my favorite food. Then I will give you God's special blessing for our family."

Rebekah overheard every word. While Esau went hunting, Rebekah started scheming.

"Hurry, Jacob!" she said. "I'll cook for your father. You trade places with your brother."

"But Mother," he said, "Father will know! Esau is hairy!"

"Just do as I say, son," she said.

So Jacob dressed in Esau's clothes. He covered his arms in goat hair and took the food to his father. It would be a slick trick.

26

"I'm back!" Jacob said, pretending to be Esau.

"That was quick," said Isaac.

"God helped me," Jacob lied.

"Come closer," Isaac replied. "You sound like Jacob, but you do feel like Esau."

Isaac promised Jacob God's blessing. There was nothing left for Esau.

Jacob had fooled his father and cheated his brother. He also had to leave his mother.

"When Father dies," Esau raged, "I will kill my brother."

Some tricks are not so slick.

27

A Sweet Dream

Genesis 28:10–22

Have you ever had such a good dream that you didn't want to wake up? Then you know how Jacob felt when God promised to keep him safe.

Jacob ran away from Esau but he couldn't run away from what he had done. He worried as he went. He wanted to go home. That night, he slept with his head on a rock — and Jacob dreamed. He saw the angels that are always around us but seldom seen. Then he saw God!

"I was with your grandfather, and your father too," said God. "I promise to protect you and always be with you. This land will be yours. Your family will be bigger than you can imagine. A Savior will come from your people and bless the whole world."

Jacob woke up amazed and thought, "I met God right here!"

He tipped the rock upright and left it there so that he would always remember God's special care.

"I will make you my God too," promised Jacob. "If you keep your promise, I will follow you."

The Colorful Coat

Genesis 37

Have you ever hurt someone so much that you felt almost as bad? That's how Joseph's brothers felt when they hurt Joseph and lied to their dad.

Joseph loved his colorful coat.

He was Jacob's favorite son and he knew it. His eleven brothers knew it too! They were green with envy. They hated Joseph's coat. They hated Joseph's dreams. They hated ... Joseph.

"In my dreams you all bow down to me!" Joseph said.

His brothers had had enough. "We'll never bow to you," they huffed.

One day, they were working in the field. Joseph was coming. They were so angry they saw red.

"Let's kill him," they said.

"Let's not," said Reuben. "We can throw him in this black pit instead."

So they grabbed Joseph, took his coat, and did just that.

As they were having lunch, some traders came by on the way to Egypt. Their camels were loaded with things to sell.

Judah had an idea. "They can sell Joseph as well!"

So they sold their brother for twenty silver coins. They killed a goat and covered the coat with blood. Jacob thought Joseph was dead. He was heartbroken.

Joseph felt sad too. He would soon be far away from everything he knew.

Prison to Palace

Genesis 39–41

Have you ever known that God has a good plan for you even when things go wrong? That's how Joseph felt even though he was in prison.

Joseph was in jail but he trusted God. He knew God had a plan. One day the King of Egypt asked to see Joseph.

"I've been having strange dreams," said the King. "Can you tell me what they mean?"

"God will tell me and I will tell you," said Joseph. "Then you'll know just what to do."

Joseph listened to the King. The King told Joseph everything.

"There were seven fat cows grazing by the river. Then seven skinny cows ate them for dinner!"

God helped Joseph to understand.

"For seven years there will be lots of food for everyone. Then there will seven years when there is none. You need a plan!"

"Joseph, I have a job for you," said the King. "You can tell us what to do!"

So Joseph got to work. While the crops were good, Joseph stored up extra food. When the crops went bad, Joseph shared out what they had. Joseph was in charge of everything and was treated almost like a king!

Sorrow to Joy

Genesis 42–45

Do you find it hard to forgive, but feel better when you do? Then you know how Joseph felt when he forgave his brothers.

When the bad years came, people traveled to Egypt from far away. Joseph's big brothers came to see him one day.

It had been a long time. Joseph looked like a King! Joseph knew his brothers, but they did not know him!

They bowed down on their knees.

"We have come to buy some food," they said. "Can you help us please?"

Joseph was amazed at this sight. He remembered his dreams. His dreams were right!

Joseph stored up lots of food, but in his heart he stored up good.

He gave them grain to fill their sacks. When they needed more, they came back. Their youngest brother Benjamin was with them too. Joseph was so happy! He just had to tell.

"It's me — your brother Joseph! I am alive and well!"
His brothers were so sorry for what they'd done.
"You hurt me. It is true," said Joseph. "But God used it for good. Now I can help you! I choose to forgive. Bring Father with you and come here to live!"

The Basket Baby

Exodus 1:22–2:10

Have you ever done just the right thing at the right time? Miriam helped to save her brother's life.

The new King of Egypt hated God's people living in his land. He was very cruel.

"Throw all their *baby boys* in the river Nile!" said the nasty King with a nasty smile.

Jochabed had a sweet little son. She sang a sweet song all night long.

"Hush little baby. Don't say a thing. We must keep you a secret from the nasty King."

But the baby got bigger as babies always do. Now what was his sweet mother to do? She made a basket and tucked him safe inside. Then she hid the basket by the riverside. Big sister Miriam kept an eye close by.

Now a pretty princess with a pretty smile often took a bath in the river Nile. She saw the basket bobbing and the baby tucked inside.

"Hush little baby. Don't you cry," she sighed. "I will love you. I will not let you die!"

Miriam saw how the princess loved her brother.

"I know someone who can help!" said Miriam. Then she went to get their mother.

Jochabed held her sweet little son and sang a sweet song all night long.

"Hush little Moses. God knows everything. You are now a prince in the palace of a King!"

Ten Terrible Plagues

Exodus 3–13

Have you ever wanted to help someone in trouble? Moses helped his people get away from the cruel king.

Moses hated how the king treated God's people. All day, every day, they were forced to work hard. All day, every day, they cried out to God.

One day, Moses saw something amazing. A bush was blazing but it didn't burn up. God spoke to Moses.

"I am going to save my people. Tell the king to set them free!"

Moses was afraid, but he did as he was told. He went to the king and said, "Let God's people go!"

"No!" said the King. "They belong to me! They don't belong to your God. I will not set them free!"

Then all day, every day, he worked them even more. All day, every day, harder than before.

So Moses went to warn the King.

"Let God's people go! There will be trouble if you say no!"

The river ran red. There were frogs, flies, and bugs. Animals died and people got sick. There was hail, fire, and darkness. Locusts ate the crops they sowed. But the King's heart grew even harder. He would not let God's people go.

Finally the King's eldest son was among many sons who died.

"Take your people, Moses. Go from here!" he cried.

Red Sea Rescue

Exodus 14

Have you ever been part of a happy, cheering crowd? Then you know how God's people celebrated when God set them free.

It didn't take long for God's people to pack. And it didn't take long for the King to want them back.

"After them!" he shouted. "Don't let them get away!"

Then all the King's horses and all the King's men chased after God's people. The King led the way.

They were almost to the sea. The soldiers were near. There was nowhere to go! They were trapped and full of fear!

"We could have stayed where we were and died!" they cried. "Why did you bring us here?"

But it was God who had rescued them; God would set them free.

Moses raised his stick — and a path opened through the sea!

The soldiers tried to follow, but the waves came crashing down. God's people were safe on the other side. None of them were drowned.

They sang their thanks to God and cheered and danced around. The praise of God's people is such a joyful sound!

Grumble, Grump, and Groan

Exodus 16:1–16, 17:1–7, 40:34–38

Do you know anyone who complains a lot? Then you know how patient God had to be with his people.

They were going to a new land. God promised it would be their own. But all they seemed to do was mumble, mump, and moan.

"We're hungry! We're tired! We're thirsty!" they whined. "We should have stayed at home."

"God takes care of us every day," said Moses. "How quickly you forget. We have manna, meat, and water. There is no need to be upset!"

God saved them from slavery. God never left them alone. But all they seemed to do was grumble, grump, and groan.

"How long until we get there?" they muttered. "We just want to go back home."

"God shows us the way every day," said Moses. "How quickly you forget. God is in the cloud and fire ahead of us. There is no need to be upset!"

God was patient with his people everywhere they roamed. God is patient with us too, even when we grumble, grump, and groan.

Loving God and Living Together

Exodus 19–20; Mark 12:30–31

Have you ever wondered how to live God's way?
God gave us rules to help us live for him every day.

God gathered his people by a big mountain.
Thunder clapped. Lightning crashed. A thick
cloud covered the mountain. The people quivered.
Moses went up to meet with God.

"I promise to make you my people," God said.
"But you must promise to do what I say."

The people promised, but it wasn't going to be
easy. They didn't know how to love God and live
God's way. So God spoke from the smoke.

"I am God. I saved you and love you very much.
Never worship idols you can see or touch.

"I am the only God. You must worship only me.

"When you say my name, say it lovingly.

44

"There are six days for working and a seventh day for rest. Remember to remember me and you will be blessed.

"Respect your parents.

"Do not murder.

"Be true to your husband or wife.

"Do not take what isn't yours.

"Don't be jealous.

"Don't tell lies."

These ten rules — the Ten Commandments — give us all a clue. God loves us. We must love God too! Treat other people as you want them to treat you.

Twelve Spies

Numbers 13-14, Deuteronomy 1

Do you sometimes worry even when you are told everything will be alright? That's what happened to God's people when they were afraid.

They were almost to the Promised Land. Moses was excited, but the people didn't know what to expect.

"We're here! Let's go and win it," said Moses.

"We're not so sure! Let's see what's in it," said the people.

So Moses picked twelve men to take a look and come back again. As the people set up camp, the spies set out to find out everything they could.

46

Caleb and Joshua came back carrying a huge and heavy cluster of grapes.

"God keeps his promises," they said. "It is a good land!"

"On the other hand," said the other ten, "the people are huge and we are small. The cities have walls that are heavy and tall."

"God is with us!" said Caleb and Joshua. "Let's go and get it!"

"We're afraid," God's people cried. "Can't we just forget it?"

God saw what was happening. He saw that his people still didn't trust him.

"After everything you've seen me do," he said, "you still don't think I'll take care of you. You are not ready to live in the Promised Land."

By the time they were, they had wandered in the desert for forty years. It's better to trust God than give in to our fears.

Joshua and Jericho

Joshua 6:1–20

Have you ever been asked to do something you didn't understand? God's people were ready to do whatever God asked them.

When Moses died, Joshua became the leader of God's people. He believed what God said. The people did too. This time they would be ready to enter the Promised Land.

"This is the plan," God told Joshua. "I want you to go to Jericho. The gate is shut tight, the walls are strong. But, if you do what I say, the walls will fall down. The walls will all fall down."

So they marched around the town, round and round the town. Once a day for six days

they marched without a sound — no one said a word. Only their trumpets could be heard. The people inside Jericho thought it quite absurd.

On the seventh day they marched seven times round and round the town. The trumpets blew! They gave a shout! Those walls came tumbling down and down. The walls came tumbling down!

49

The Thankful Smile

Ruth 1–4

Have you ever felt so loved that you were thankful and smiled? That's how Naomi felt when she held her new grandchild.

Naomi's husband and two sons had died. She looked at her daughters-in-law one day.

"I am old," she said. "I can do nothing for you. You should go back to your own families."

Orpah was sad — but she went on her way.

Ruth said, "I will not leave you all alone. I will go with you — your God will be my own."

Naomi was thankful — and she smiled.

They went to live in Bethlehem where Naomi had lived as a child.

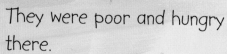

They were poor and hungry there.

"I am old," she said. "I can do nothing for you."

But Ruth said, "I will care for you. I will gather grain. Trust God. Life will be good again."

Naomi was thankful — and she smiled.

Boaz owned the fields. He saw Ruth working hard every day.

"She takes care of Naomi and is very kind," said a worker. "She gathers the grain we leave behind."

"Naomi must love her very much," Boaz said.

Then Boaz began to love her too.

Naomi was thankful — and she smiled.

Boaz and Ruth became husband and wife. They cared for Naomi the rest of her life. She did trust God and life was good again. When they had a baby son — she was thankful and smiled.

The Listener

I Samuel 3

If you have ever wondered what God wants to say to you, then you know how Samuel felt when God woke him up.

Young Samuel lived in God's house with old Eli, the priest. He was learning how to serve God.

It had been a busy day. Samuel was a sleepy boy. He went to bed and closed his eyes. He heard someone calling.

"Samuel."

He rose and ran to Eli.

"Here I am," said Samuel.

"I didn't call you," Eli said. "Go back to bed, sleepy head."

Samuel closed his eyes. Then he heard his name again.

He rose and ran to Eli.

"I'm here," said Samuel.

"I didn't call," Eli said. "Go back to bed."

Samuel closed his sleepy eyes. A third time someone called.

He rose and ran to Eli.

"Here I am," said Samuel.

"God is calling you," said wise old Eli. "Next time, tell him you're listening."

Samuel went off to bed. Soon he heard God calling again.

"Samuel! Samuel!"

"I'm listening," Samuel said.

God often spoke to Samuel and Samuel grew wise. Samuel never stopped listening to God. We are all wise when we listen.

The Mightiest, Frightiest Giant

I Samuel 17

If you have ever been the youngest and the smallest, then you will know how David felt when he beat Goliath!

Goliath was the mightiest, frightiest giant God's people had ever seen. He wore giant armor and held a giant sword. He also had a giant voice.

Every day he shouted, "I'm the biggest giant you ever did see. None of you is brave enough to come and fight me."

And because no one was, their enemies were winning.

Now David was the youngest and the smallest of his brothers. He was also the bravest. One day, he heard Goliath boasting.

"I'm not afraid," David said. "I'll fight that big bully."

"You're too small," said God's people. "At least put on some armor!"

But David chose his shepherd's sling.

"You can't beat Goliath with that thing."

"I can't," David said, "but God can!"

And off he went to fetch five stones and face Goliath. It only took one. It hit Goliath on the head and the giant fell down dead.

God's people cheered. Their enemies ran away. God is the mightiest and the greatest.

The Kingmaker

1 Samuel 8–10, 15–16

Have you ever judged someone by the way they look? Then you'll know how Samuel felt when God asked him to anoint a king.

Samuel helped the people listen to God, but they wanted a king instead.

"Everyone else has a king," they said.

"We're not like everyone else," said Samuel. "God is our King."

Samuel spoke to God. God was sad too. "They are rejecting me; they are not rejecting you."

God helped Samuel choose a king, even though he knew the trouble it would bring. King Saul was quiet, handsome and tall.

"Long live the king!" the people cheered.

"Love God and obey him!" Samuel warned.

When King Saul wouldn't, God helped Samuel choose someone who would.

"He will be one of Jesse's sons," said God.

Samuel thought God would choose the oldest. He was tall like Saul.

"No," said God. "He's not the one at all."

God chose David, the very youngest instead. He took care of sheep, played the harp, and loved God with all his heart.

"One day David will be king. He loves me more than anything," God said.

Good looks aren't everything.

The Wise King

1 Kings 3:5–15, 8:54–66, 10:1–29

When Solomon became the king, God said, "Ask me for anything."
What do you suppose Solomon wanted most of all?

"Anything?" asked the king.

"Anything," answered God.

Solomon liked gold. He liked to win battles. He liked the idea of living a long life. But he loved God. He wanted to be a good ruler and make good choices.

"I don't know anything about being a king," said Solomon. "So what I'd like best of all is to be wise."

God liked Solomon's answer.

"You will have wisdom," God said, "and fortune and fame! Everyone will know your name!"

And so they did! Even the Queen of Sheba who lived far, far away!

Solomon made good choices, gave good advice, and he made a grand temple for God's people to worship in. They had a great festival to celebrate.

"God is good!" Solomon said. "God keeps his promises!"

Solomon was wise to praise God's name. We can be wise and do the same.

Just Enough

1 Kings 17:8–16

Have you ever wondered how God will take care of you? Then you will be amazed by how he cared for Elijah, the widow, and her son.

There was too much sun and not enough rain. There was not enough grain to make bread. There was not enough water to drink.

God sent Elijah to a woman for help. She was out gathering firewood when he came. They were both hungry and thirsty.

"May I have some water and bread?" asked Elijah.

"I have just enough flour and oil to make bread for one last meal," she said. "Then my son and I will die."

"God will take care of you," said Elijah.

So the kind woman gave him some water and baked him some bread. The jar of flour should have been empty — but it wasn't. The jug of oil should have been empty — but it wasn't.

From that day on until there was just enough rain, she had just enough flour and oil over and over again.

The Little Hero

2 Kings 5:1–15

Have you ever wanted to tell a grown up about how God can help them? Naaman's servant girl wanted to help her master get better.

Everyone tried to be kind, but General Naaman knew they were looking at him. His skin was blotchy and itchy. There was nothing any doctor could do.

"I know someone who can help!" said the girl who served his wife. "Elisha will ask God to heal him and it will change his life."

So Naaman saddled up his horse and went to Elisha's house.

Naaman was a hero. But he felt like a nobody when Elisha didn't even come to meet him. Elisha sent a messenger instead.

"Wash seven times in that river and you will be well," he said.

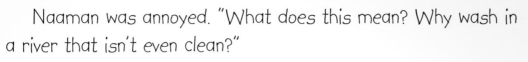

Naaman was annoyed. "What does this mean? Why wash in a river that isn't even clean?"

"If you believe what God says," said Naaman's servant, "maybe you can be well."

So Naaman washed seven times. When he was done, his skin was as good as new!

He ran to Elisha and said, "I know your God is true!"

He thanked Elisha and tried to pay him in gold.

"No," said Elisha. "God is the real hero."

And so was the little servant girl, if the truth be told.

63

The Big Fish

Jonah 1:1–17, 2:10

Have you ever wished that you said yes the first time you were asked to do something? Then you know how Jonah felt when he was swallowed by a big fish.

"Jonah, go to Nineveh," God said. "Tell them I see the bad things they are doing. I want them to change."

God said, "Go!" but Jonah said, "No!" He was afraid and jumped on a ship for far away.

While Jonah slept, a storm stirred. Thunder crashed. Lightning flashed. The sailors were scared.

"We're going to sink!" they screamed.

The captain shook Jonah. "Wake up! Do something! Pray!"

"It's my fault," said Jonah. "I'm running away from God. Throw me into the sea and you will be safe."

So they did.

64

The storm stopped. The sailors were saved. So was Jonah.

Glub, gulp, swish, swish. Jonah was swallowed by a great big fish! He had time to think. He had time to thank God and pray.

"I'm truly sorry for running away," he told God. "I will keep my promise to do whatever you ask."

The big fish burped. Jonah bounced on to a beach. Jonah got a second chance.

Mission Accomplished

Jonah 3:1–4:11

Have you ever wanted someone to get into trouble? Jonah wanted God to stay cross with the people of Nineveh.

Jonah told the people of Nineveh that God was cross with them. He thought they should get into trouble.

"God says to change your wicked ways or else!" Jonah said.

He never thought they would. But they did! They were truly sorry and showed it. They asked God to forgive them and help them.

God gave them a second chance too.

Jonah was cross. "I knew you would

66

forgive them," he sulked. "It's so unfair after all the bad things they have done."

He sulked his way out of the city and sat on a hot hill.

God gave Jonah a tall shady plant. Jonah was happy. The plant died. Jonah was upset.

"You loved your plant even though it was just a plant," God said. "I love people. Shouldn't you?"

God forgives us when we are truly sorry. We should forgive others.

The Fiery Furnace

Daniel 3

Have you ever been asked to do something wrong and said, "No!"? Then you know how it felt for Shadrach, Meshach, and Abednego.

King Nebuchadnezzar made a huge golden statue. He told everyone to bow down and worship it or be thrown into a flaming furnace.

Shadrach, Meshach, and Abednego said, "No!"

"Bow down," fumed the King, "or into the fire you'll go!"

They would not do what they were told.

"You are great," they said, "but God is greater still! If God wants to save us, we know he will. We will worship God alone, not a statue made of gold!"

The furnace raged, the King raged hotter; he turned up the heat seven times higher! The men were tied up and tossed into the fire.

The King gazed into the blaze. He was amazed.

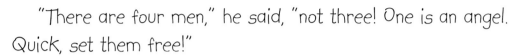

"There are four men," he said, "not three! One is an angel. Quick, set them free!"

They were unhurt, unafraid, unsinged, and untied.

"You don't even smell like smoke!" the King cried.

He told everyone that God alone could save.

"A king is great, but God is greater still. God will be with us in everything."

Claws, Jaws, and Silly Laws

Daniel 6

Do you like to talk to God and ask for his help every day? Daniel loved God and liked to pray.

Daniel lived far from home but he was close to God. Day in, day out, three times a day — Daniel knelt by his window to pray.

King Darius knew that Daniel was wise and honest. He trusted Daniel's good advice. This made the king's other advisers jealous. They knew that Daniel was a praying man, so they devised a nasty plan.

"King, live forever!" they said. "Here's what to do. Everyone should pray only to you! Anyone who doesn't should be arrested and then thrown into the lions' den!"

The king liked this law a lot. He forgot about Daniel — but his advisers did not.

Day in, day out, especially that day — Daniel got down on his knees to pray. He asked God to be near him and then — Daniel was thrown into the lions' den.

The king couldn't sleep that night. He ran to the den in the morning light.

"Daniel!" he cried. "Did your God save you?"

"King, live forever!" Daniel said. "I'm alive too. Day in, day out, God is near. He sent an angel to keep me safe in here."

"No more claws and jaws and silly laws," said the King. "We will ask God's help with everything!"

71

Good News!

Matthew 1; Luke 2:1–20

If you have ever waited a long time for a promise to come true, then you will know why so many people were happy when Jesus was born.

An angel came to see Mary — she was surprised.

"Don't worry," said the angel. "God has chosen you! There is nothing God can't do. You will be the mother of God's own Son. He will show people how to live for God, and he'll forgive them the wrong they've done."

When an angel came to see Joseph, he was surprised.

"Don't worry," said the angel. "God has chosen you, too! You will marry Mary and help her raise God's Son. He will show people how to live for God, and he'll forgive them the wrong they've done."

When it was almost time for the baby to be born, Mary and Joseph traveled to Bethlehem. They tried to find a place to stay, but all the inns were full that day! People here, people there, all kinds of people everywhere!"

"Don't worry," said an innkeeper. "You can stay in my barn."

So Mary and Joseph did their best to settle down and have a rest. It wasn't long until the time had come! Mary had a baby son. They named him Jesus. It means "God saves."

Shepherds' Delight

Luke 2:8-20

If you have ever been given good news, then you will understand why the shepherds just had to share it!

It was quiet on the hill that night. Some shepherds were watching their sheep nearby. Suddenly they saw a dazzling light.

"Don't be afraid," an angel said. "I bring you good news with great delight! A baby was born today and is lying in a bed of hay. He is the one God sent to save."

Before the shepherds could think what to do, many other angels gathered there too. They all praised God and began to sing, "Glory to the newborn King! Peace on earth for everyone!"

Then as quickly as they came, the angels were gone. The shepherds stood there all alone. They looked at each other, they looked at their sheep. They knew they'd never get to sleep.

The shepherds were filled with such delight they ran to town that starry night! They found the babe where the angel had said, snuggled up warm in a manger bed: the one God sent to save.

They smiled at the baby fast asleep. Then they went back to the hill to take care of their sheep. They sang praises to God all through the night and spread the good news with great delight.

A Wonderful Adventure

Matthew 2:1–12

Do you know anyone who says kind things they don't mean? King Herod pretended to be kind, but he was really mean.

"There's a new star!" said the wise men. "Where's the new king?"

And off they went on a new adventure. They followed the star far away, wondering as they went. When they got to King Herod's palace they wondered out loud.

"Where's the newborn King?" they asked. "We saw his star from afar and want to worship him!"

When King Herod heard, he was most upset.

"I don't want to be the old King yet!" he stomped.

"God promised a special new King," his advisers said. "Everyone is waiting for him. He will be born in Bethlehem."

King Herod had a nasty plan to kill the new King. He called the wise men.

"When you find him," he said sweetly, "you must tell me too so I can worship him just like you!"

When they did find Jesus, their smiles were as bright as the star. They knelt on their knees and gave him gifts — gold, incense, and myrrh.

King Herod waited, but the wise men did not go back. God sent them a new way home, wondering about the new King as they went.

Temple Talk

Luke 2:41–52

If you have ever wanted to learn more about God, then you know why Jesus enjoyed being in the Temple.

Jesus wasn't lost. Not really. He knew exactly where he was. But his parents didn't. They were lost in worry. The streets were crowded, and they had been looking frantically, asking everyone, shouting everywhere for three days. They couldn't sleep. They couldn't eat. They couldn't think of anything else.

Finally, they found him. He was talking with the teachers in the Temple. He was lost in his thoughts about God. The teachers were amazed at how wise he was for a twelve-year-old. His parents were amazed too.

"Jesus!" Mary cried. "Where have you been? We have been looking everywhere for you!"

Tears filled her eyes. Jesus looked surprised.

"I didn't mean to worry you," he said. "I've been here in my Father's house. I thought you knew."

"We're just so glad to see you, Son!" they said hugging him.

"I'm glad to see you too," Jesus said. Then they all went home.

Jesus obeyed his parents as he had always done. He pleased God his Father and grew up wise and strong.

Jesus Is Baptized

Matthew 3:13–16 Mark 1:9–13 Luke 3:1–20

Have you ever waited for a special person to arrive? Then you know how John felt when he waited for Jesus.

John was preaching loud and clear.

"God's promised one will soon be here! Love God! Live God's way! God's kingdom is near!"

People were sorry for the wrong they had done. They wanted God to forgive them. John wanted them to show this by being baptized in the river.

"This is only water," he said. "The one who is coming will baptize you with the Holy Spirit instead!"

Then one day, Jesus came to be baptized. John knew he was the one!

"It's me that needs to be baptized by you!" said John.

But Jesus said, "Let's do what pleases God."

When Jesus came out of the water, the heavens opened. The Holy Spirit settled on him as gently as a dove.

"I love my Son so much," said a voice. "I am happy with everything he does."

First Followers

Matthew 4:18–22; Mark 1:16–20; Luke 5:1–11

Do you believe in Jesus and want to follow him? Then you know how Jesus's first followers felt.

It was morning. Peter, Andrew, James, and John had *been* fishing all night and not got a nibble. Now they were washing their nets.

There was a crowd on the beach listening to Jesus teach.

"Everyone can *be* part of God's Kingdom," he said.

The crowd got bigger and bigger. Jesus got into Peter's boat and they *bobbed* away from shore.

"God loves you! Love God too! Live God's way and love others the way that God loves you!"

When Jesus was finished, he turned to Peter and said, "I feel like fishing!"

"I've already been," said Peter. "Not a nibble."

"Let's try again!" said Jesus. So they did.

Suddenly, there were more fish than a fisherman could wish for. The nets were bursting!

"Come and help!" shouted Peter to the others.

Soon both boats were so full they began to sink! Peter began to think. He fell to his knees and said, "Lord, I've done so many wrong things!"

"Come on," Jesus said to them. "Follow me and we'll fish for people until God's Kingdom is bursting!" And they did.

The Man on the Mat

Matthew 9:1–8 Mark 2:1–12 Luke 5:17–26

Have you ever needed help from your friends? The man on the mat needed his friends too.

Jesus was preaching. The house was packed. People could hardly move.

The man on the mat couldn't move at all. But he had four friends who carried him where he needed to go.

"Let's go and see Jesus," they said. "He can help you!"

"How can we do that?" said the man. "No more people can get through the door."

The friends had a chat.

"Who needs a door? The roof is flat! We'll knock a hole through and lower you."

"Good plan," said the man.

"Where there's a will, there's a way," said his friends.

The friends carried the man on his mat. They climbed on to the roof that was flat. They knocked a hole through and lowered him down to Jesus.

Jesus looked at the man amazed. Then he looked up at his friends and smiled. He saw faith in their eyes and hope on their faces.

"All will be well," he said. "Your sins are forgiven," he said to the man, "and you can walk!"

The man carried his own mat.
He jumped, skipped, and walked
by himself.

How to Pray

Matthew 6:7–13; Luke 11:2

Have you ever wondered how to talk with God? Jesus's friends wanted to know how to pray too. Jesus taught them what to do.

"Keep it simple. Use your own words. Mean what you say. God knows how you are feeling even before you pray.

"Talk to God as a loving Father who wants what is best for you. You are God's child. God wants to be with you.

"Remember God's name is holy and what God says is true.

"Ask God to be the king of everything. Pray that God will help you do what he wants you to.

"Pray for the things you need to live.

"Ask him to forgive you and to help you to forgive.

"Pray that God will keep you safe — and help you choose to live his way."

How Not to Worry

Matthew 6:19–7:12

Do you want to trust God more and worry less?
Listen to what Jesus says.

Jesus was teaching on a hillside. It was a lovely day. The birds were singing. The flowers were blooming. But people were worrying as people often do.

"Don't worry about what you will eat or drink or wear," said Jesus. "Just look at the birds in the air. They don't sow seeds for food to eat. God takes care of all their needs.

"Will worrying make you stronger or help you live longer?

"See the flowers that grow? They don't sew their own clothes but they are more beautiful than King Solomon's robes.

"God loves you even more than the birds and the flowers.

"There's more to life than fashion and food. God will take care of you. God is good.

"If you look for something, you find it. If you knock on a door, someone answers it. If you ask your parents for bread, do they give you a rock instead? Ask God for the things you need and you will receive. God is good. Do you believe?

"Don't put your trust in the things that you own. Things are easily lost or stolen or worn. God's treasures last for ever. Gather these and you will have all that you need.

"Worry doesn't change a thing. Trust God for everything."

Two Builders

Matthew 7:24-27, Luke 6:47-49

Have you ever tried to build something only to see it crash to the ground? Then you know how the builders felt in this story Jesus told.

"There were once two builders. Each of them wanted to build a house. The first builder was wise. His plan was sound. He chose to build on solid ground. He dug down deep and laid a firm foundation. The work was hard and long, but the house he built was sturdy and strong. When the rain lashed down and the floods flashed up, the house on the rock withstood the storm. Those who do what I say, and live God's way, are like this.

"The second builder was foolish. He had no plan. He chose to build on sandy land. The house looked grand and went up fast. But when the rain lashed down and the flood flashed up, the house didn't last. It crashed! Those who promise to do what I say, but don't, are like this.

"Don't call me your Lord unless you mean what you say," said Jesus. "Those who follow me must live God's way."

The Soldier's Servant

Matthew 8:5-13 Luke 7:1-10

Have you ever known for certain that you would get what you asked for? A Roman soldier knew that Jesus could be trusted completely.

One day, an officer from the Roman army rushed up to Jesus.

"Please help!" he begged. "My servant is in pain and can't move his legs! I know that you have the power to heal."

Jesus could see that his faith was real.

"I will come right now and make your servant well."

"You don't need to come," the officer said. "You can make him better from just where you are. I tell my soldiers what to do and they obey. You can command sickness to go away. Just say the word."

Jesus was amazed by what he heard.

"I have never found so much faith in anyone! Not even in Israel! Go home. Your servant will be well."

And he was.

The Most Important Thing

Matthew 13:44–46; Mark 12:30–31

Have you ever wondered what God wants us to do most? Then you know why someone asked Jesus this question.

Jesus traveled from town to town. He showed people how to love God and live God's way. One day, a man was listening.

"What is the most important thing God wants us to do?" the man asked.

"God loves you completely. Love God completely too!" Jesus answered. "And treat other people as you want them to treat you."

"I understand," said the man. "I should give my love to God before I give him any other thing."

"Yes," said Jesus. "Treat him as your King."

Jesus often told people what God's Kingdom is like.

"God's Kingdom's like a treasure hidden deeply underground. When you find it, you *sell* everything to buy it — and all the ground around.

"God's Kingdom is like the most precious pearl on earth. You'd give your whole life for it. That is what it's worth."

The more you give yourself to God, the more you know it's true: God's Kingdom is not just in heaven — God's kingdom is in you!

The Churning, Turning Lake

Mark 4:35–41

If you have ever wanted a storm to stop, then you know how it felt when Jesus calmed the lake.

It wasn't stormy when they set out, but it was now! The wind churned and turned. The waves churned and turned. The boat churned and turned.

Jesus wasn't worried, not one little bit. He was sound asleep in the back of the boat. His friends were about to sink to the bottom of the lake! The boat tossed up and down.

"Wake up, Jesus," they said. "We're going to drown!"

Jesus stood and stretched out his hand.

"Keep calm," he said to the churning, turning wind.

"Keep calm," he said to the churning, turning waves.

"Keep calm," he said to his churning, turning friends. "Why are you so afraid? Trust me and you can be brave."

The storm stopped.

Now they had a churning and turning question. "Who is this man that even the wind and the waves obey?" they asked. Jesus's friends thought only God could do that.

We know only God can!

A Fabulous Feast

Matthew 14:13-21; Mark 6:30-44; Luke 9:10-17; John 6:1-15

Have you ever been worried you didn't have enough to share? Then you know how Philip felt.

Thousands of people had been with Jesus and his friends all day.

"It's time to eat," Jesus said to Philip. "Where can we buy them some bread and meat?"

"Are you being funny?" said Philip. "We don't have much money. And we'd never find enough food for everybody!"

But Jesus knew what he was going to do.

"Ask around the crowd," he said to his friends.

A little boy stood beside Andrew.

"You can have my lunch," he said.

"It's only two fish and five pieces of bread," said Andrew.

"Is everyone sitting down?" Jesus smiled. "Let's eat!"

Then Jesus thanked God for the food they all shared. There was plenty for everyone with more to spare.

Everyone was amazed by what Jesus had done.

The crowd began to whisper, "He's the Promised One!"

When they followed him the next day, Jesus said, "People need bread to eat, but they need God's Word even more."

99

Waterwalkers

Matthew 14:24–33 Mark 6:48–52 John 6:16–21

Have you ever succeeded at something you thought you'd never be able to do? Peter walked on water when he kept his eyes on Jesus.

The sea was rough. The rowing was tough. Jesus's friends were in trouble. Suddenly, they saw something in the night. They were terrified.

"There's a g-g-ghost coming toward us!" they cried.

"Take courage," said Jesus. "It's me."

"If it's really you," said Peter, "let me come to you."

"Come on," said Jesus. "You can walk on water too!"

Peter stepped out on to the sea. He kept his eyes on Jesus. Everything was going well. But when he heard the wind, his fear swamped him. He looked down and began to drown.

"Save me, Lord!" he cried.

"Your faith is so small," said Jesus. "Why did you doubt?"

He took Peter's hand and helped him out.

They got back into the boat. The wind stopped. The sea was still. They were safely on the shore. Everyone was amazed by what Jesus had done. They worshiped him and said, "You are God's Son!"

The Good Neighbor

Luke 10:25–37

Have you ever been helped by someone you didn't expect would help you? Then you know how the traveler felt in this story Jesus told.

"A man was traveling on a lonely road. He walked up a hill. When he got to the top he stopped.

"Suddenly some robbers hit him on the head, left him half dead, and took everything he had.

"A priest walked up the hill. When he got to the top he saw the man but didn't stop.

"A temple helper walked up the hill. When he got to the top he didn't stop either!

"A stranger from another country went up the hill on a donkey. But when he got to the top, clip clop, he stopped and hopped down.

"'Poor man!' he said and bandaged his head.

"He put the man on his donkey and led the donkey down the hill. He took the man to an inn and cared for him. When he had to go away for awhile, he paid the innkeeper to take care of the man."

Now Jesus had a question for the people listening to him.

"Who was the good neighbor and what did he do? You must be a good neighbor too."

The Busy Sister and the Big Meal

Luke 10

Have you ever been so interested in something that nothing could distract you? Then you know how Mary felt when she was listening to Jesus.

Martha and Mary were happy when Jesus and his friends came to visit. While Martha got busy making a feast, Mary sat and listened at Jesus's feet.

Martha scrubbed, peeled, diced, and sliced. Mary didn't. Martha measured, mixed, kneaded, and baked. Mary didn't. Martha set the table and poured the wine. Mary didn't.

"It's not fair," Martha puffed. "I'm doing all the work," Martha whined. "I've had enough!" Martha huffed. "I'm being busy!" she said to Jesus. "Mary is being lazy! Will you ask her to help?"

"Dear Martha, can't you see?" Jesus smiled. "Mary is spending time with me. While you have been busy cooking all day, Mary has listened to all I say."

We are blessed when we spend time with Jesus.

The Good Shepherd

Matthew 18:12-14; Luke 15:3-7; John 10

Have you ever found it hard to love someone? God loves everyone — even the people we might find it hard to like.

"If a shepherd has a lot of sheep and one sheep leaps away, he leaves them all safe on the spot and searches for the one that got away. He will look here and there and everywhere. He will walk and climb and run. Day or night, he will never stop until he finds that one. He brings the sheep home safe and sound, and leaps for joy that his sheep is found.

"Heaven has a happy day," said Jesus, "when anyone chooses to live God's way.

"I am the Good Shepherd," Jesus said. "I know all my sheep by name.

"No matter where they wander, I love them just the same. I will give my life to save them, no matter what the cost. If you want to follow me, you must love the people who are lost."

God loves everyone — no matter what they're like.

Ten Men Well Again

Luke 17:11-19

Have you ever been bursting with excitement at a very special gift? Then you know how a man with leprosy felt when Jesus made him better.

Ten men wanted to be well again. They saw Jesus passing by.

"Jesus, help us! Please!" they cried.

Their faces were full of scars and their skin full of sores. They couldn't live with their families anymore. Jesus felt their pain.

"Go and show the priest your skin," said Jesus. "You will all be well and can go home again."

As the ten men began to go, their skin got better! They ran off happily. Only one man ran back to thank Jesus for healing his disease. He praised God and fell down on his knees.

"Thank you, Jesus," he said.

"I made ten men well again," said Jesus. "I am glad you said thank you."

Jesus is glad when we thank him too.

The Power over Death

John 11

Have you ever been sad when someone died? We can understand heaven better because Lazarus came back to life.

When Lazarus died, Jesus cried. Even though he knew it would happen; even though he knew he could have stopped it. People were crying together because they missed Lazarus so much.

"Where were you?" sobbed Martha when she saw Jesus coming. "My brother died! If you had been here to make him better, he would still be alive!"

"Everyone dies, Martha," Jesus said softly. "But it isn't the end. Everyone who believes in me will one day live again. Do you believe?"

"I believe you are the one that God promised to send," said Martha.

Martha went to get Mary. Mary ran to Jesus. She fell at his feet and cried.

They took Jesus to the tomb where Lazarus was buried.

"Roll the stone away," Jesus said.

Everyone was surprised.

"He's been dead for four days!" said Martha.

"I have power over death,"
Jesus said.

Everyone held their breath.

Jesus prayed that they would believe
in him. Then he called loudly, "Lazarus, come
out!"

And he did! He was alive!

"Take him home," Jesus said with a smile.

Mary and Martha cried again — this time with
joy. Many people *believed* in Jesus that day.

The Honest Man's Prayer

Luke 18:9-14

Do you sometimes feel bad about the things that you do? God loves you and is waiting to hear from you.

Jesus told this story to some people who thought they were better than others.

Two men went to the Temple to pray. One man thought he was better than the other. He stood up proud and prayed out loud.

"Thank you, God. I am so good. I always do the things I should. I share my money. I keep the rules. I spend my time in prayer. I'm not like that man over there."

The other man knew he wasn't always good. He didn't always do the things he should. He hung his head and sadly said, "Forgive me, God, for the things I've done. I know that I'm the guilty one."

Which prayer do you think God answered?

"If you pray for show, God will know," Jesus said.

When you pray from your heart, God will always help you.

Jesus Blesses the Children

Matthew 19:13–15, Mark 10:13–16, Luke 18:15–17

If you have ever felt that grown-ups don't have time for you, then you will be glad to know that God always does.

114

Jesus was busy. People needed his help. They called out to him and crowded around him everywhere he went. They wanted Jesus to heal them with his touch. But some people who came to see him didn't need very much. Parents wanted Jesus to bless their children and pray. But his friends thought they were a bother and said, "Go away!"

"Jesus has too much to do," they said. "He has no time to spend with you."

When Jesus heard this, he was upset.

"That's not true!" he said. "Let the children come."

He talked with them and blessed every one.

"God's Kingdom is full of children," he said to his friends and smiled. "If you want to get into God's Kingdom, you must trust me like a child."

A Blind Man Sees

Mark 10:46–52

Have you ever been given what you asked for and more? Jesus gave Bartimaeus his sight and a whole new life.

The coming crowd was very loud. Bartimaeus could hear them walking. He could hear them talking. But he couldn't see them. Bartimaeus was blind. He sat begging by the side of the road.

"What's going on?" he called out. "Who is there?"

"Jesus is coming," someone finally said.

Bartimaeus began to shout, "Jesus! Help me!"

"Hush! Shush! Be quiet!" said the crowd.

But Bartimaeus didn't listen. He just shouted louder, "Jesus! Over here! Help me!"

When Jesus heard, he stopped and turned. "Tell him to come to me," he said.

"Cheer up! Get up! Come on!" said the crowd. "Jesus is calling you!"

Bartimaeus jumped to his feet and felt his way to Jesus.

"What do you want from me?" Jesus said tenderly.

"Teacher!" Bartimaeus said. "I want to see!"

"Go!" said Jesus smiling. "Your faith has given you sight! Open your eyes!"

Suddenly Bartimaeus could see everything. He could see everyone. And Bartimaeus could see Jesus!

"I can *see*! I can *see*! I can *see*!" he shouted happily.

"He can *see*! He can *see*! He can *see*!" the crowd cheered.

Bartimaeus joined the crowd along the road, but it was really Jesus he followed.

The Little Man and the Big Change

Luke 19:1-10

Have you ever thought that someone will never change? When Zacchaeus met Jesus, he began to live God's way.

Lots of people crowded around Jesus. Everyone wanted to see him and hear what he said. Zacchaeus wanted to see him too. But no matter how hard he tried — he couldn't see over and he couldn't see through. He was just too small.

"I can't see Jesus at all," said Zacchaeus. "But I can see a tree."

So he climbed up to get a good view. Jesus got a good view too.

"Come down, Zacchaeus," Jesus said. "I'd like to spend some time with you! Let's go to your house."

It turned out that Jesus knew more about Zacchaeus than his name. Zacchaeus had his own kind of fame. He was rich because he took money that didn't belong to him.

"He's a cheat!" said the people to each other.

"I want to change!" said Zacchaeus to Jesus. "I will give half of all I have to those who are poor. And if I've cheated anyone, I will pay them back — and four times more!"

"Zacchaeus! You have been saved today!" Jesus said. "I came to help people to live God's way."

Here Comes the King

Matthew 21:1–11; Mark 11:1–70; Luke 19:38–40; John 12:12–19

Have you ever been so happy you just had to cheer? Then you know how the crowd felt when they welcomed Jesus to Jerusalem.

Jesus and his friends were walking to Jerusalem. When they were almost there, Jesus said, "There is a donkey in the next town. No one has ever ridden it. Find it and bring it here."

Now the donkey didn't buck when Jesus sat on his back. It didn't kick or bray — not even when the crowd scattered their coats along the way.

People waved palm branches in the air. There was so much celebration! Almost everyone began to cheer!

"He is coming! Jesus is here!"

Some people were not so happy. They didn't like what Jesus did or said. They were angry. They didn't believe that Jesus was the one God sent.

"Stop their cheering!" they said to Jesus. "What's this nonsense all about?"

"I could keep them quiet," Jesus smiled, "but the stones would still cry out!"

121

Dusty, Dirty Feet

John 13:1–20

Have you ever had someone tell you what to do? Jesus doesn't just tell us, he shows us.

It had been a dusty day. It would soon be time to eat. Jesus and his friends had dirty feet. Jesus filled a bowl with water and began to wash each one. Then he dried them with a towel as a servant would have done.

"I can't let you wash my feet, Lord!" Peter said. "That's not your job to do!"

"Everyone is a servant in my kingdom," said Jesus. "If you want to be part of it, you must let me serve you too."

"Don't just wash my feet then!" said Peter. "Wash my hands and my head!"

"Oh Peter, the rest of you is clean!" Jesus said. "I just need to wash your feet, my friend."

Then Jesus asked them all, "Do you understand what I have done for you? Show your love by serving others as I have served you."

The Special Supper

Matthew 26:17–29; Mark 14:12–25; Luke 22:7–20; John 13:18–30

Every time we go to Mass, we celebrate the special gift of the Eucharist that Jesus gave us. He is always with us.

Jesus was eating with his friends. But he was thinking about what would happen to him soon.

"Some people hate me," Jesus said. "They don't believe God sent me. They are going to kill me."

"We won't let that happen!" said Jesus's friends.

"It already is," said Jesus. "One of you has even promised to help them find me."

They were shocked! They wondered who it might be. Judas slipped out of the door quietly.

Jesus took some bread and broke it. He thanked God and gave it to them.

"This is my body," he said. "It is broken for you."

Then he poured some wine. He thanked God for it and gave it to them.

"This is my blood," he said. "It is poured out for you.

"I am going to die, just as it was written, so that people can be forgiven. But I am also going to live again and go home to my Father in heaven. One day, you will come too. Every time you eat and drink this," said Jesus, "remember that I love you and have given my life for you."

In the Garden

Matthew 26:31-55; Mark 14:27-52; Luke 22:39-54; John 18:1-12

Have you ever felt very alone? Jesus knew what it was like to feel alone and for his friends to let him down. He understands when we feel scared.

It was dark outside. Jesus felt afraid. He needed help to be brave. He asked his friends to go into the garden with him and pray.

Jesus told them, "You will all deny me or desert me before the night is through."

"Not me!" said Peter. "It can't be true!"

"Yes," said Jesus, "even you. The rooster will crow twice at dawn. You will say that you don't know me three times by then."

"I will never deny your name!" said Peter. "I would die first!" And all the others said the same.

Jesus's friends fell asleep. Jesus prayed all night long.

"I am your Son," he said to God, his Father. "I will do what must be done!"

Light flooded the garden. A crowd came with torches, swords, and clubs. Judas came with a kiss.

"Friend," said Jesus. "Are you betraying me like this?"

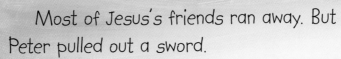

Most of Jesus's friends ran away. But Peter pulled out a sword.

"Put it down," said Jesus calmly. "Angels could save me if I called. But who would save you then? I am the Lord."

Peter Denies Jesus

Matthew 26:69–75; Mark 14:66–72; Luke 22:54–65; John 18:15–27

If you have ever let a good friend down, you will know how Peter felt on that dark night.

Peter was afraid, but he followed just the same. He wanted to know what would happen. He wanted to be close to his friend. While soldiers took Jesus inside a house, Peter stood outside, warming himself by a fire. A servant was looking at him.

"You were with Jesus!" she said.

Peter looked surprised.

"Who me?" he answered. "No!"

Just then, a rooster began to crow.

A little while later another servant said, "I'm sure you are one of his friends."

"I don't even know him!" Peter lied.

"You talk just like him," someone else replied.

"I tell you," Peter swore, "I do not know the man!"

And even as he said it, the rooster crowed again.

Peter knew he had broken his promise to be true. He was so sorry he felt his heart was breaking too.

Just then, the guards took Jesus by. Jesus turned to Peter and looked him in the eye. Peter felt so ashamed that he cried.

Jesus Dies on the Cross

Matthew 27, Mark 15, Luke 23, John 19

No one shows greater love than being willing to die for a friend. Jesus died even for those who hated him.

Jesus did not hate those who hated him. He did not hate those who told lies about him. He did not hate those who ordered him to die. He did not hate those who beat him until he *bled* or pushed a thorny crown onto his head. He did not hate the soldiers who led him to the place where he would *be* killed. He did not hate them when they nailed him to a cross.

He did not hate the people who *stood* there on the hill.

"If you are the one God *sent*, come down from the cross," they jeered. "You can't even save yourself. How can you save us?"

Jesus did not hate his enemies. He loved them instead.

"Father, forgive them," he said.

Many who loved Jesus were also there. They watched and wept and waited. It took long hours for Jesus to die. The sky went dark.

"My God, my God," Jesus cried, "why have you left me all alone?"

When the time had come Jesus whispered, "It is done!"

Then Jesus died for everyone.

The Empty Tomb

John 20:1–18

Has anyone ever promised you something that seemed impossible?
Jesus keeps his promises.

Mary was sad. She walked to Jesus's tomb in the dim light of dawn. But the stone was rolled away! The tomb was empty! Jesus was gone! She ran straight away to tell Peter and John.

"Someone has taken Jesus's body!" she cried.

Peter and John couldn't believe it. They ran to the tomb, side by side. The only things they found were the grave clothes Jesus had been buried in.

Mary stood crying all alone when they had gone. When she looked into the tomb again, there were two angels where Jesus's body should have been.

"Why are you crying?" the angels asked.

"I can't find Jesus!" Mary said through her tears.

Then she thought she saw the gardener standing near.

"Did you take Jesus?" she asked him. "Please tell me where."

"Mary," said the man.

Mary stopped and stared for she knew him then. It was Jesus! Jesus was alive again!

"Go and tell the others that I am alive," Jesus said.

Mary could hardly believe it! It was such a surprise! She ran and told Jesus's friends, "Jesus is alive — and I have seen him with my own eyes!"

Thomas Believes

Luke 24:36–49; John 20:19–29

Do you have trouble believing what you haven't seen for yourself? Then you know how Thomas felt.

Jesus's friends were afraid. They met behind locked doors. Suddenly Jesus appeared and said, "Peace be yours."

They thought he was a ghost!

Jesus showed them his hands, his feet, his side. Then they ate together.

"It's true! It's you!" they cried.

"Just as the Father sent me," he said, "I am sending you. The Holy Spirit will come. He will help you do what I would do."

Now Thomas wasn't there when Jesus appeared.

"Thomas!" they said. "We have seen the Lord!"

"I will not believe," said Thomas, "unless I touch his wounds for myself."

A week later, Jesus's friends were together as before. Suddenly Jesus was there again and said, "Peace be yours."

Then he said to Thomas, "Touch my hands and side. Have faith and believe — be satisfied."

Thomas didn't need to touch him!

"My Lord and God," was all that he could say.

"You believe in me because you have seen me," said Jesus. "Happy are those who have never seen but believe in me anyway."

Do You Love Me?

John 21:1–14

Do you find it hard to forgive yourself when you hurt someone? Jesus forgave Peter and wanted him to forgive himself too. Jesus had work for Peter to do.

It was morning. Peter and some of Jesus's friends had been fishing all night and not got a nibble. The last time this happened, Jesus filled their nets and Peter left everything to follow him. Now Peter didn't know what to do. He had denied even knowing Jesus. He felt disappointed in himself and thought Jesus would feel the same.

Suddenly, a man on the shore gave a shout. "Catch anything?"

"Not a nibble," Peter shouted back.

"Try again, friend!" he said.

Something felt familiar. Peter and his friends put their net back in. Suddenly, it was full of fish. The feeling grew. John said, "It's Jesus!" Suddenly, Peter knew too!

"Jesus! It's Jesus!" he shouted as he jumped in and swam to shore!

Jesus was cooking breakfast on the beach.

"Where's the fish?" he asked, smiling at Peter.

Soon Peter helped the others drag the net to land. Everyone was so happy. It was the best breakfast ever.

"Peter, do you love me?" asked Jesus.

"Oh, you know I do!" said Peter.

"Then take care of my friends — and love them as I have loved you."

Home to Heaven

Matthew 28:16–20; Mark 16:15–20; Luke 24:44–53; Acts 1:6–11

Have you ever been given a really important job to do? Jesus told us to help others believe in him.

Jesus met with his friends often. They spent time walking and talking and eating together. They were happy that Jesus was alive! They felt brave having him near. But now it was time for Jesus to go home to heaven. They met together one last time.

"God has given me power over earth and heaven," Jesus said. "It's your job to tell everyone everywhere the good news. Everyone can be my friend. All can be forgiven.

"Teach people to believe in me and to live God's way. Whenever you worry or wonder, remember I'm with you always.

"You must wait now in Jerusalem. The Holy Spirit will come. He will give you all the power you need to do what must be done."

Then Jesus went into heaven. He was surrounded by clouds. His friends couldn't stop looking at where he disappeared. They didn't know what to do or say!

Then two angels appeared. "Why are you standing here looking sad?" they asked. "He'll be back again someday."

The Holy Spirit Comes to Help

Acts 2

Do you find it hard to live God's way? Ask the Holy Spirit to help you every day.

Jesus's mother and his friends were in Jerusalem. They were waiting and praying for the Holy Spirit to come. Suddenly, there was a sound like a rushing wind. Then something like a small flame of fire settled on each one. They knew the Holy Spirit had filled them. They began to speak in languages they'd never heard before!

Jerusalem was filled with visitors from all over the world. They were astonished by what they heard. Jesus's friends were speaking and they could understand every word!

"How can this be?" said many. "This is very odd! They are speaking to me in my own language about the love of God!"

"They are out of their minds," said others.

140

But Peter was bold and told them about all that Jesus had done.

"We can all be forgiven for the things we do wrong. God sent Jesus to save us. God loves everyone!"

Thousands of people believed in Jesus and were baptized that day!

They met to worship God, to share their belongings and to pray. They asked the Holy Spirit to help them live God's way.